HOW TO BASECAMP

Your Power to Convene,
Your Courage to Begin Again

CHRIS KUTARNA

NEW GEO
NEW THINKING TOGETHER

10 9 8 7 6 5 4 3 2 1

NewGeo Press
House of Ideas, Ltd
Highbury, London N5 2PD

www.newgeo.org

A CIP catalogue record for this book is available from the British Library.

Paperback ISBN: 978-1-0682013-0-1

eBook ISBN: 978-1-0682013-1-8

Typeset in Gaultier by R Ward

Illustrated by Potion Creative

Printed and bound in Great Britain

For permissions or bulk-purchase inquiries: contact@newgeo.org

For you

and the journey of discovery that only you can instigate

Where do you feel the strain
most strongly...

between the world as it IS
and the world you ACHE FOR

...even if you don't know how to
change it?

Contents

if you've just been invited to someone else's Basecamp, read this!

Acknowledgements

This guide is a product of massively collective effort and intelligence.

Thank you, first and last, to the 2,732 people (more or less!) who took part in Basecamp:Toronto (2018), Basecamp:London (2019), the over 20 public Basecamp@HOME events hosted throughout the COVID pandemic (2020-2022), and the many private Basecamps hosted with institutions, corporations, and project teams across North America, Europe, and Asia. Every iteration made these pages clearer.

This guide could not exist without the contributions of the organizing team around those inaugural Basecamp events — especially Scott Annan, Leah Andrews, and Casper Jorna — who poured heart, mind, and soul into audacious acts of convening.

Don Simpson is one of the brightest lights in the sky, shining with the truth that convening is a profound act of leadership — and a voyage of discovery. Jay Jennings generates a field of conviction, which deepens the actions of everyone in his radius. Robert Poynton is a courageous creator of new spaces for thinking and feeling in brave new ways. Fodé Beaudet is a profound learning partner, whose insights into how to hold multicultural, multi-sectoral dialogue and inquiry are informed by decades of professional practice doing exactly that at the highest levels.

A pantheon of people have all left indelible marks upon these pages: Yabome Gilpin-Jackson, Alex Jadad, Glenda Eoyang, *both* Nicholas Parkers, Simon Lau, Margaret Heffernan, Sophia Ikura, Tracey Camilleri, Cassandra Kelly, Adam Grodecki, Lynn Lilley, David Tullett, Steve Mostyn, Sarah Thomas, Pan Xiaoli... Apologies for the glaring omissions too numerous to list. Each in their own practice, they help people in small groups to big governments get grounded, think deeper, see clearer, stay truer to their intentions, elevate dignity, and be more human.

Special thanks to: Rachel Ward, whose creative team at Potion Creative dove into designing this Special Edition of *How To Basecamp* with a gusto that delighted everyone involved; Dustin Moore, head of Ivio Agency, whose brand partnership has been instrumental for turning complex ideas into stories that resonate; and New Geo's Research Director, Piotr Schulkes, whose brilliance astonishes.

Most importantly, thank you to my wife, Maximilia, for your steadfast belief in the importance of words strung together with good intentions.

London, 2025

"THIS IS A DRAFT. PLEASE HELP TO IMPROVE IT WITH YOUR EXPERIENCES."

Chris Kutarna

Intro - We need to brave new ways

THIS IS A GUIDE FOR BRAVING NEW WAYS TO A NEW WORLD.

It is the collective, living output of a global community of inquiry, who share a commitment to finding new ways to think, act, and be.

Although we travel different paths, we're all coming to the same realisation: we need to brave new ways.

For some of us, the path to getting here has been an **inward** journey: a growing recognition of stress and fatigue, of fragmentation and disconnection, of schedules too full to do what matters most, of minds too busy to reflect upon the new choices we might make.

For some of us, the path here has been an **outward** journey. The global financial crisis. Democracy in crisis. A global pandemic, and other pandemics underway still struggling for recognition — like mental health or public debt. The side effects have now become the main result. Solving crises of our own making has now become society's primary occupation.

Some of us have come to this realisation from the **past**. Outdated ideas, norms, institutions or habits keep frustrating the ways we want to travel. Our horizons keep expanding, but obsolete maps try to trap us onto familiar avenues of thought, action and being.

Some of us have come to this realization from the **future**. It's a future that is less hierarchical and more networked. Less about extraction and more about creation. Less about flows of oil and more about flows of photons. The coming years may be the most transforming in all human history. We can reach a new world of abundance. But it won't simply arrive. We'll have to achieve it.

From all these directions — inward and outward, past and future — we are coming to a common conclusion: *making progress now is not simply a matter of more or faster, but differently.*

A VERY BASECAMP BELIEF

"If we speak with each other as humans, we will figure it out. We can have [redacted] conversations and build societal structures that evolve beyond the limitations of the past."

SHOULD YOU BRAVE A NEW WAY?

"Begin where you are."

Here is the list of situations we've found so far, where going a brave new way improved the situation and led to better outcomes.

Do any of these situations feel familiar to you?

- You or your team has begun to ask unsettling questions. (In this guide, 'unsettling' is a good thing. It is the sentiment that '*We can't stay here*' or '*We can't stay on this path we've been going*.' Questions that arise from this sentiment inspire movement.)
- You've begun to worry about what's in your blind spots. You fear you're failing to see something big, but you don't know what it is.
- You see no clear path forward, or no good options.
- You or your team feel distanced or disconnected from what really matters.
- You feel that too much time, energy, and human potential is sucked into serving the needs of the organization instead of serving a significant Purpose.
- You want people to feel that they bring their whole selves to work, but you or your leadership have doubts about how to navigate the tensions between 'what interests me' and 'the organization's interests'.
- You're looking for a way that can't simply be looked up, a way that other people can't simply tell you (no matter the knowledge or expertise they might have compiled). You're looking for a way that hasn't yet been found.

If you identify with one or more of these situations, and you are ready to move past it, this guide may help you make an unexpected journey of discovery.

A word of warning: Do not tread lightly. There is a comforting familiarity about each of the above situations. This guide is intended to help you leave them behind, and find new ways. Are you ready?

Then let the journey begin.

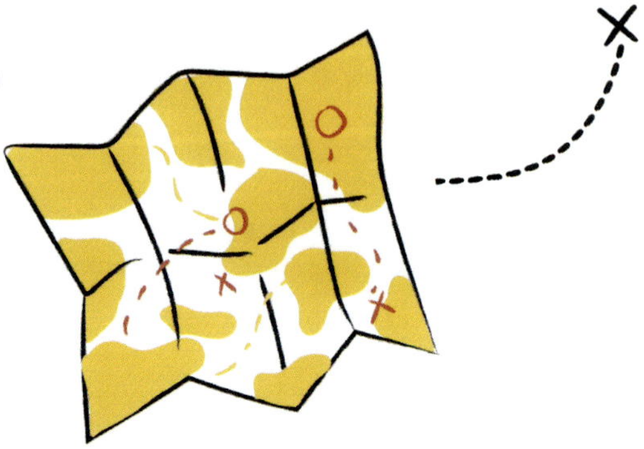

HOW TO USE THIS GUIDE

This guide will set you on a journey.

The journey begins inside you, with your realization that '*There's gotta be another way...*' to deal with the important thing you're dealing with. This guide will take you up to the point where you are surrounded by diverse others who are ready to join you in braving a new way.

Where that journey takes you is beyond the scope of this particular document. The aim of this guide is to help you get to that brilliant beginning with other people whom you have inspired to come together.

This guide has three parts:

1. *Part I, Make Your Map*, takes you from that first moment of realization to the point where you have mapped out the topic as you currently see it and are ready to share how **you** see things with the rest of the world.
2. *Part II, The Power of Convening*, helps you figure out who to invite to join you on this journey, how to invite them, and how to sense and signpost the stuff you must explore together. By the end of Part II you will have inspired a group of individuals who are all eager to meet up and discover what they might learn by learning together.
3. *Part III, Where Brave New Ways Begin*, helps you to create, hold, and curate the space where those discoveries happen.

This guide is a gateway to human help.

This guide is the output of hundreds of in-person and virtual experiments to explore better ways of bringing forth the collective intelligence needed to navigate a new world.

But there is no one right way to brave a new way; this guide may or may not be the right way *for you.*

So this guide is also your invitation to tap the skills and experiences of a global **community of inquiry** that is emerging around these methodologies — and many others like it, and some very different.

If you would like help adapting these approaches to your unique context, NewGeo can be your gateway to a global, eclectic community of thinkers and practitioners: skilled learning partners in every country who can accompany you, your organization, initiative, or community, large or small, along your own journey: from questioning, to consequences, and back.

THIS GUIDE IS A GATEWAY TO HUMAN HELP

NewGeo is a society for brave rethinkers.

It's a global, eclectic community of inquiry for people who sense that the old maps are broken — and are ready to explore what comes next.

Through workshops, convenings, custom cohorts, and thought leadership, we help you challenge assumptions, stretch perspectives, and translate new ways of seeing into meaningful action. Together. Because no one person can reimagine the future alone.

We create the conditions for you to discover new worlds — and lead us there.

Inquire deeper, at **newgeo.org**

YOU ARE BEGINNING SOMETHING BIG

I wonder
what's under here...?

Part 1, Make Your Map....

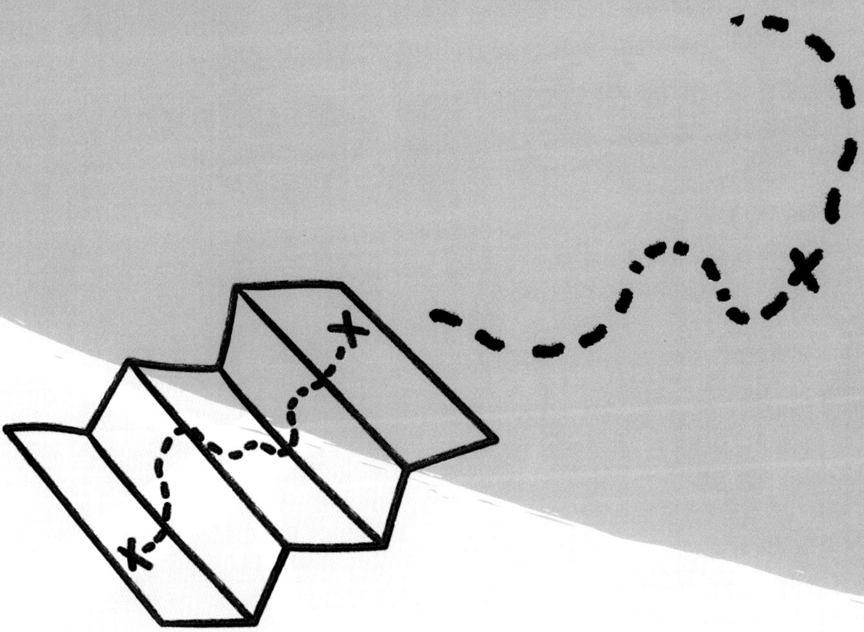

PRINCIPLES OF MAP MAKING

This journey starts by drawing your map — by sketching the world as you see it now. You can do it yourself, or as your team. Your map will make plain, to you and one another, the territory that needs to be explored **between you**.

Unlike most maps (and most documents!), **your goal is to *never* arrive at the finished version**. You want this journey to reveal new horizons. You want what you see now to keep changing, keep expanding, and keep challenging what you saw before.

When you're done drafting your map, you will hold in your hands a compelling *Call to Basecamp*. Just by looking at it, you yourself will already see many new paths you want to explore more. Other people will be eager to point out things that you can't see.

That's why you will invite them to join you (at a place you call Basecamp) to improve your picture together and begin new journeys of common purpose toward shared horizons.

EXPLORE, DON'T CONQUER

When drafting your map of the territory you see, it is important to reveal what you don't know. By doing so, you invite others to do the same. The better you can set that tone, the more revelations your own initial draft will evoke from other people, and the bigger the discoveries you'll make together.

Speaking from our own painful experiences, maps full of authority and expertise fail to inspire journeys of discovery. (But they're great for getting people to follow us to places we've already been.)

LESS IS MORE

Draft with the intention to leave your work unfinished.

Keep in mind:

1. You're not trying to be the last word; you're trying to start a new conversation.
2. Every section you leave unfinished, you create an opportunity for other people to finish it differently than you might have — maybe in ways that reveal to you important things you couldn't see.
3. Too much information can be confusing to people who don't breathe the same air as you.

In each section, aim for a minimum of three bullet points and a maximum of ten. (More information can be given in appendices or weblinks, for those who wish more detail.)

To draft your map, you need to sketch five things about the territory you want to explore:

1. Give the Context
2. Name the Challenges
3. Signpost Pathways
4. Bring Beliefs to the surface
5. Declare your Intentions

The following pages will help you do each of these steps. And then you'll have taken things as far you can on your own. You'll have a map. It'll be in draft. And it'll be time to identify and convene the people who can best help you keep it that way.

YOUR BLIND SPOTS ARE A GIFT

Life is impossibly rich with information. As single individuals, we cope by simplifying *what is real* down to a manageable chunk, called *what is real* ***to me***. We condense what seems to matter most into a picture we can understand, or a story we can relate to. We filter out what seems irrelevant or inconsistent. We focus on the things that seem to fit best with the rest of the picture we've built up in our heads.

In short, we try to sort the signal from the noise. We start to make sense of what is happening, because we believe we see the key relationships of cause and effect. And it seems to work. We gain the power to influence outcomes.

Then a global pandemic happens.

By sketching out your own map, you make plain to others what you can't see.

And that's what you want to do. Your aim here is to reverse your own reductive processes: to remove some of the filters you unconsciously apply to everything, to unfix your mental models, to challenge the wisdom you assume to be true or timeless, in order to discover the wellspring of all new possibilities: your own blind spots.

YOUR BLIND SPOTS ARE A GIFT.

They are pathways to new knowledge, new connections, and new ways. Find them and share them.

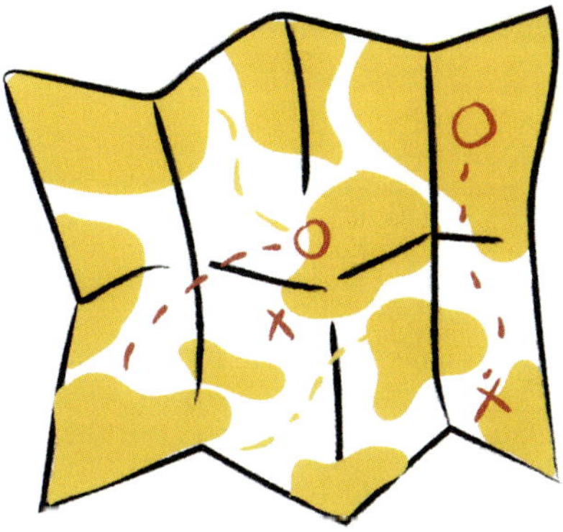

HOW TO DRAFT YOUR MAP

The purpose of your draft is not to defend a position, but rather to capture your understanding of a topic and your relationship with it, and lay that out for others to explore with you.

It's meant to serve as a starting point for reflection and discussion, as an example of being transparent about how you experience a situation, and as an invitation for other people to add to your picture with their understanding, challenges, assumptions, and desired outcomes.

STEP 1 GIVE CONTEXT

Start by sketching your **Context**, because this part of your map is often closest to the surface and the easiest to describe. "What's going on out there?"is a question we often ask ourselves. So: What is going on out there?

- What's the situation, as you see it?
- What's the story you tell yourself about where we are?
- What are the factors, events, or developments that you point out, to explain why we're here and how we got here?

Begin to notice (and try to describe in a few bullets) the narrative you have learned to tell about the situation you are in: where you are, why you are there, and what it looks like.

If you like to think in a structured way, there's a rich universe of tools and templates out there to help you describe your Context systematically. Here's one that we've found useful. Just don't feel bound to complete it, or to obey its logics.

FOUR REALITIES

STEP 2 NAME CHALLENGES

If Context is how you see your world, **Challenges** is how you describe your agency in it. We are all the heroes of our own story. Given the world that you've described, what heroic labors need doing?

What odysseys or obstacles do you see for you and for the people trying to navigate your Context?

The shift from describing "Context" to describing "Challenges" is, incidentally, what happens in meetings whenever somebody asks, "So what?" Wisely or foolishly, what they are really saying in that moment is, "I have heard enough about the Context. I get your story. Now, tell me about my role in it."

In particular, try to name:

- **Opportunities for Action:** What needs to change? To be tested? To grow? To be asked? To be explored?
- **Costs of Inaction:** What might the outcomes be, if action isn't taken to meet these Challenges you see?

Again, use a template like this one if that helps you locate your own thoughts and feelings better. Just bear in mind: Your task here is not to fill in someone else's boxes. Your task is to log whatever is arising most strongly for you.

FOUR POSSIBILITIES

Not all those who wander are lost.

- J.R.R. Tolkien

STEP 4 BRING BELIEFS TO THE SURFACE

Everything you've described so far is **filtered** by your own assumptions about what is real, how the world works, and what matters most. Some of your assumptions, you're aware of.

Most of them, you're not.

At Basecamp, you will discover that other people (who come at the world from a different perspective) find it really easy to point out to you the assumptions you don't realise you're making.

But doing it ourselves can be quite hard. Imagine if for your Context, you had drawn a literal map of a physical territory: a continent full of mountains and forests and great cities, and then an ocean, and on the other side of the ocean the vague outline of an island you still know little about. The Challenge is clear: to explore that island. And the Pathway is clear, too: to cross the ocean, somehow.

But then you meet someone from a coastal Arctic civilisation. For them, the land is featureless (snow) and the sea teems with opportunity, and you realise something: the ocean is more than a chasm to cross; it is a whole new world of its own.

Aha!

Having our assumptions pointed out to us can be incredibly powerful. It can lead us to discoveries that help us ask better questions, tackle better problems, and make better decisions.

Frankly, it'd be easier to let other people list your **Beliefs** for you. So why do it yourself, if others can do it better? *Because of the signal it sends.* Your beliefs are personal things. We're now getting into the parts of your map that are hard to separate from your own sense of self. The conversations you convene will be as brave or as safe as the example you set here.

Of course, there is no end to your own list of beliefs. Stroll through the philosophy department of any good university, and the faculty there will gladly burden you with a million unexamined beliefs about the world you didn't know you rely upon every day.

So the task here (as with any map) is to communicate what you think is *relevant*. It's okay not to get existential. Focus on the Beliefs you see within the Context and Challenges and Pathways you've described so far.

Once other people join you around your draft, the list of relevant beliefs will probably grow. (And if it doesn't, that'll be a sure sign that you're still missing important perspectives.)

Just remember you're trying your best to put on the table not just what you see, but **how you see** the world. You're showing people how to do that, so that they'll do the same.

Be as brutally honest with yourself as you can here.

It will pay off greatly.

Organize your Beliefs however you wish, or not at all. One structure we've found helpful for compiling some of your key beliefs is:

- Beliefs about **your own** role or place in the world
- Beliefs about **other** peoples' motives, role, or place in the world
- Beliefs about how you and they are connected or related or **interact**
- Beliefs about how you'll interact and respond to one another **in this process**

HERE ARE A COUPLE OTHER QUESTIONS THAT COULD HELP:

* What beliefs do you hold about your topic that you tend not to voice?

* What are some beliefs others hold that you think are different from yours?

STEP 5 DECLARE YOUR INTENTIONS

The last step is to sketch out your personal **Intentions**.

Why are you going through this process? Why is this important to you, your group, or community?

This piece is vital. Putting your motives into this picture is your way of saying,

"I don't think this is a simple problem that we can just step back from, analyse objectively, and solve the way we've solved problems in the past. I think ***how*** *we think and act may also be part of what makes this situation. We can't step back from it; we're in it. And to improve it, we probably need to improve our understanding of the part we play in it."*

For many people, declaring your intentions might be the most **unsettling** part of your picture — in a good way.

People know how to react to a SWOT analysis; it produces fairly predictable conversations and outcomes. People don't quite know how to react to the stuff you'll do right here. It **unfixes** them from rehearsed ways of interacting with you. And therein lies the opportunity for fresh paths to emerge.

Just as with your beliefs, there is an endless list of revelations you might make here. You have an entire life story, and without your complete story no one can completely understand you. True. But that's not this. In our experience, there are five most relevant bits about yourself that are relevant to reveal right now:

- **Motivations:** Why are you doing this? What drew you here, and what keeps you here?
- **Skin in the game:** What's at stake for you in this?
- **Feelings:** What affects you in this (at a feeling level)? What doesn't affect you?
- **Hopes and Fears:** What about your own future feels enabled or threatened?
- **Energy:** What gives you energy in this? What steals your energy away? What do you have energy to do more of?

Go through this list, and offer a few bullet points of personal revelation that you think will help others to understand why you have drawn this picture for them and why you have taken the time to draw it.

One of the clearest lessons drawn across the whole history of Basecamp is: we tend to underestimate the power of being vulnerable upfront.

Apply that lesson here.

For example, Chris tells this story...

"Not too long ago, I hosted a corporate annual retreat. After the CEO had stood up and painted his vision to the team, I asked him for his **doubts** as well. What **didn't** he know about where to go and how to get there?

He answered, honestly, about some things that might really rock the boat in the near future. Then I surveyed the room and asked his team:

"How does that make you feel, when your leader says 'I don't know'?"

Their most common response?

"**Reassured**."

Leverage your own humanity to draw people into a deeper conversation with you.

It will help you all to arrive at a more valuable and meaningful outcome.

WHEN IS MY DRAFT DONE?

There is no perfect answer. The question is a contradiction!

In practice, we have found that if you run through the following three questions and you feel the energy to go **forward**...then go forward.

1. Does my map attempt to describe a territory? (Basically, am I just rambling or venting here, or have I made some real progress naming a topic or terrain — at least for myself?)
2. Have I placed myself in it? Have I disclosed or revealed at least one thing that could help other people to understand **my** connection to this topic? This stuff matters to me. Have I tried to say why?
3. Have I realized a need to convene? Or do I really just want to convince others to see things my way? (It's an honest question: the right answer depends on the context.)

(If you feel the energy to go **back**...then go back.)

LEADING WHILE LOST

You've sketched out your map of the territory. Now, what energy do you want to bring to it? Do you want to **conquer** that territory — or **explore** it?

If you've made it this far, you've probably noticed a tension growing inside you. The more you've thought about this topic from different angles, the more attuned you've become to your own energy to do something about it.

Right now is a crucial crossroads when the way you choose to go will shape everything that follows. Having sketched out a terrain, how are you now going to express **leadership**?

The most common expression of leadership at a moment like this is to use your map to *point the way forward*. "This way everyone! Follow me!"

However, because you've drawn your map the way you have, you've unlocked a different mode of leadership: *leading while lost*.

You don't want followers; you want fellow explorers. "Our ways aren't working. So what am **I** missing?" You want to invite other people to join you around your picture and help you see what you can't see.

Now may be a brilliant moment to experiment with this latter kind of leadership. Leading people down the path you can already see may be far less significant than sparking the discovery of new ways that none of you can see alone.

So take one more good look at your map and judge this territory you have described.

Do you mean to conquer it, or do you mean to explore it?

Do that gut check, and if your honest answer is "explore", then it's time to convene people around your draft.

Part II, The Power of Convening

YOU HAVE THE POWER TO CONVENE

In this next stage of the journey, you'll enrich your draft with a mix of perspectives that, right now, are **missing** from it. This rich mix won't be random. It will be other people who are related to your topic in important ways — and in ways that are different from your own. Your act of convening will serve two big purposes:

1. **To bring forth collective intelligence.** Your map will mutate into a better, more widely shared picture of the situation you're in. If you follow this guide, outcome #1 is pretty much assured.
2. **To discover new ways that can only be found together.** Some of the people who come together will discover new ways. Although they might see some things on the map very differently, they will nonetheless discern a direction they feel pulled to explore more together. And even though their destination will be unclear, they will commit to take first steps in that direction together. Adventurers might call them *scouting parties*.

In our experience, this second outcome is likely, but it's not assured.

Nor is it assured that, if scouting parties do form, you will count yourself among them. New ways may emerge that you yourself feel no energy to move towards.

You should decide for yourself right now that **that's totally okay**. What you are instigating here is going to grow into something much bigger than you. Of course, you have your own reasons for doing all this, which you have tried to make plain in your draft. But your actions here are also **a gift**.

And it's a substantial gift, because this next stage of the journey is going to demand a fair bit of work, patience, and bravery on your part.

Convening is the act of creating a deliberate time and space for a brave conversation into unknown and unsafe territory. Right now, that conversation is missing from the world, but you will cause it to exist by investing some of your energy into making it happen.

CALLING ALL EXPLORERS

You've got your map. It's only a draft. It's incomplete in some ways that you're keenly aware of — and in other ways that you don't yet realize.

Your objective now is to draw to you other people who can help make your map better.

But you're not looking to bring together just anybody.

"What's missing from my picture? What blind spots am I revealing, by framing the situation this way? What limitations am I putting on myself, before I even begin to take action?" You want to bring together people who have good responses to these questions and who are willing to offer those responses constructively toward forming a better, common understanding. You want to arrive at an improved, shared map — possibly a very different map than the one you offered as a first draft: a new map that inspires all sorts of joint expeditions that might never be conceived otherwise.

You are inviting other people onto this journey because **you cannot draw this new map alone**.

Right now is another moment when it's useful to gut-check:

Do you really believe that?

If you don't, the people you invite are going to know it. You won't get what you really need from them, because they will sense that you don't really think you need their perspective. They might suspect that your real motivation here is to gain followers.

***Followers* are people who don't question your map. They are pointless to this process.**

Do not invite followers.

Do invite **fellow explorers**.

SOME THINGS, WE CAN ONLY SEE TOGETHER

To help people feel genuinely invited on a joint journey of discovery, it helps to have some humility about how much you can ever know by yourself.

Some of the typical ways people think about knowledge can trip up your efforts to co-create an improved understanding here.

For example, you and your invitees will probably be familiar with this first picture, which divides all knowledge into three pie slices: What You Know, What You Don't Know, and What You Don't Know That You Don't Know. It presents you a neat, complete set of possibilities, and it suggests that the best way to grow knowledge is to keep growing that first slice, What You Know.

But that slice labelled What You Know? That's actually What You *Think* You Know — and maybe you don't.

What You Don't Know? That's really What You *Think* You Don't Know — and maybe you do.

And that third slice you're trying to shrink? The more you think you know, the bigger that slice is going to get!

So that top picture, while familiar, is **exactly backwards** for what you're trying to do here.

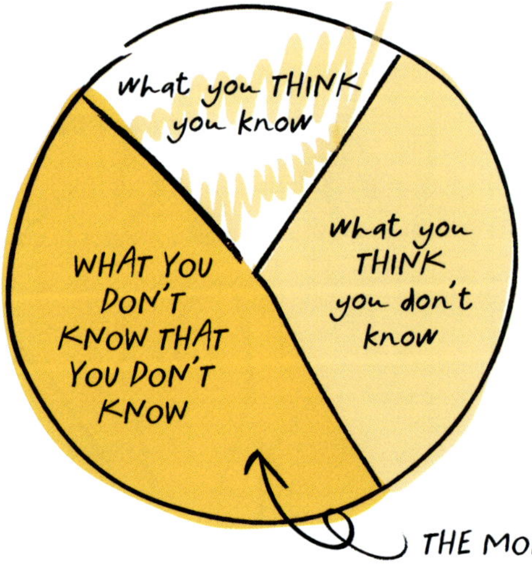

A CURE FOR "IMPOSTER SYNDROME"

Maybe you feel a little nervous about reaching out to other people who know more about your topic or territory than you do. The common term for this feeling is "imposter syndrome". It arises from picturing knowledge this way:

An intimidatingly big circle represents all that you **could** know on this topic (but don't). And then there's a small circle inside it. It wouldn't intimidate anybody. It represents the depressingly minor fraction of knowledge on the topic that you've managed to accumulate for yourself. You hope no one discovers the true size of your small circle, because (as the picture implies) you probably ought to know more than you actually do — especially if you're instigating this whole journey. In fact, you should stop right now, and leave this process up to the experts, i.e., the people whose circles of knowledge are bigger than yours. What is the value of your input when weighed against theirs, huh?

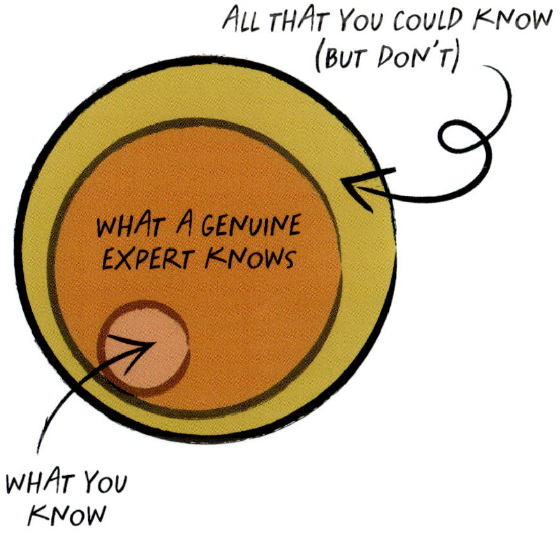

* This entire narrative is ENTIRELY WRONG for what you're trying to do here. *

Here's a different picture of knowledge that will serve you and your invitees better...

Think of the total pie of knowledge about your topic as a **ring of interlocking circles**. From where you stand in that ring, you look out and see some things that no one else can. Other things, you can't see without the benefit of someone who's standing somewhere else. The size of your own circle is not the most important thing in this picture. However big your own circle, you'll never see your whole situation alone.

This picture invites experts to link arms with you, with the same humility that led you to extend your hands to them, and look outward together. The more deeply you can see in one direction, the more rooted you are in your own perspective — and the harder it becomes to see things the way others in the circle do.

Do invite topic experts. If they are wise, as well as knowledgeable, they will see the wisdom in accepting your invitation.

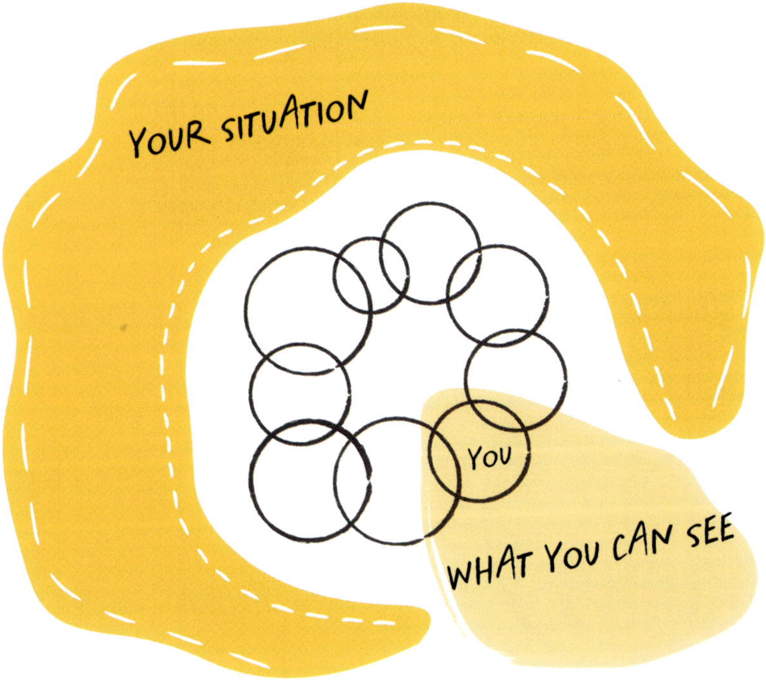

WE ARE NOT TALKING ENOUGH

Some people are going to greet your invitation with skepticism. Maybe cynicism is a better word. We've all been in conversations that went nowhere. We've all been to conferences that failed to inspire. We've all heard talk, talk, talk that doesn't seem to change anything.

Less talk, more action!
Let's get to the "So what?!?"

These phrases have the force of popular wisdom behind them, and your invitation to people to join you on this journey directly challenges that "wisdom". You are inviting people to believe, in effect, **We are not talking *enough*.**

You are inviting people to perceive that whenever we get together to act, to "solve the problem", we may be making the mistake of starting out at the wrong point. We are already **too far down** the path. We have already missed important ways we might take.

Yes, we are all eager to arrive at magnificent new solutions. But by beginning badly, we have already doomed ourselves to arrive at predictable and familiar destinations instead.

That's why what you're doing, right here right now, is so important.

BEGIN BETTER

You are inviting people to begin better. That is the hope you are selling. That is the reason to believe that you are offering to your invitees. That's what intrigues them to show up at the new starting point you have prepared: to see where they might eventually arrive if they start **differently**.

To get your invitees to suspend their skepticism, you need to demonstrate that this beginning **is** different. Better? Time will tell. But different? Definitely. Thanks to you.

Your draft map is full of thoughtful differences.

Your next act of difference-making comes right now, in how you choose the people you'll invite to join you at this new beginning.

This is another point in the process where you gift your unique perspective on your topic to the world. Whomever you choose to invite, **only you** can compile this list. Only you have the relationships to convene this unique web of perspectives.

You are the genius of this journey.

Only you can instigate it. Whatever follows from this point on is, in part, an expression of your uniqueness.

Don't let this get to your head; stay humble. But it's true. And it's a gift you are making. It's full value can never be calculated.

(We think: it's a lot. So let us be the first to say: *Thank you.*)

THE MIX THAT'S MISSING

We've learned that a reliable way to help your invitees suspend their skepticism and believe that this beginning will be better is to:

1. Recognize how a list of invitees *normally* gets drawn up, then
2. Explicitly *challenge* those ways.

Call the list you'd normally draw up "the usual suspects". You don't want to invite the usual suspects.

You want to convene **the mix that is missing**.

The precise meaning of that label is going to take some work on your part. It's going to be quite specific to your topic, your situation, your network. In general, you want to go on this journey with people outside your usual circles — people who can help you to explore what's important to you, in a wider context of what's also important to them.

We have noticed a few common models that people follow (often unconsciously) in order to arrive at a boring list of the usual suspects. If you challenge these models while compiling your list, the people who show up will be much closer to the mix that is missing. And if you make your logic transparent in your invitation, then your invitees will think so, too...

BLUNT STAKEHOLDER MAPPING

In organizational settings, whenever you talk about getting a wider group of perspectives together, people immediately think "stakeholders". For a typical corporation, stakeholders might include shareholders (of course), union and employee representatives, local government, environmental groups... You know, stakeholders.

All good. Makes sense. Who all is being affected by this situation I'm describing? Who has a stake in this topic? We need to talk to them.

And — good news! — that's already being done. A lot. Stakeholder conversations are already happening. Maybe even routine.

But surprisingly, all the routine stakeholder engagements in the world have not resolved *your* topic.

No, that's not surprising at all.

With your invitation list, you have a chance to challenge the routine. Do some **blunt stakeholder mapping**. Look at your stakeholders on this topic and ask yourself two simple questions:

- Who tends to show up?
- And who tends not to?

If it helps, group your stakeholders into the four boxes below. You might consider the righthand boxes to be "the usual suspects." Make sure to include people from the lefthand boxes on your list of invitees. If you can get the lefthand side to show up, that would already make a big difference.

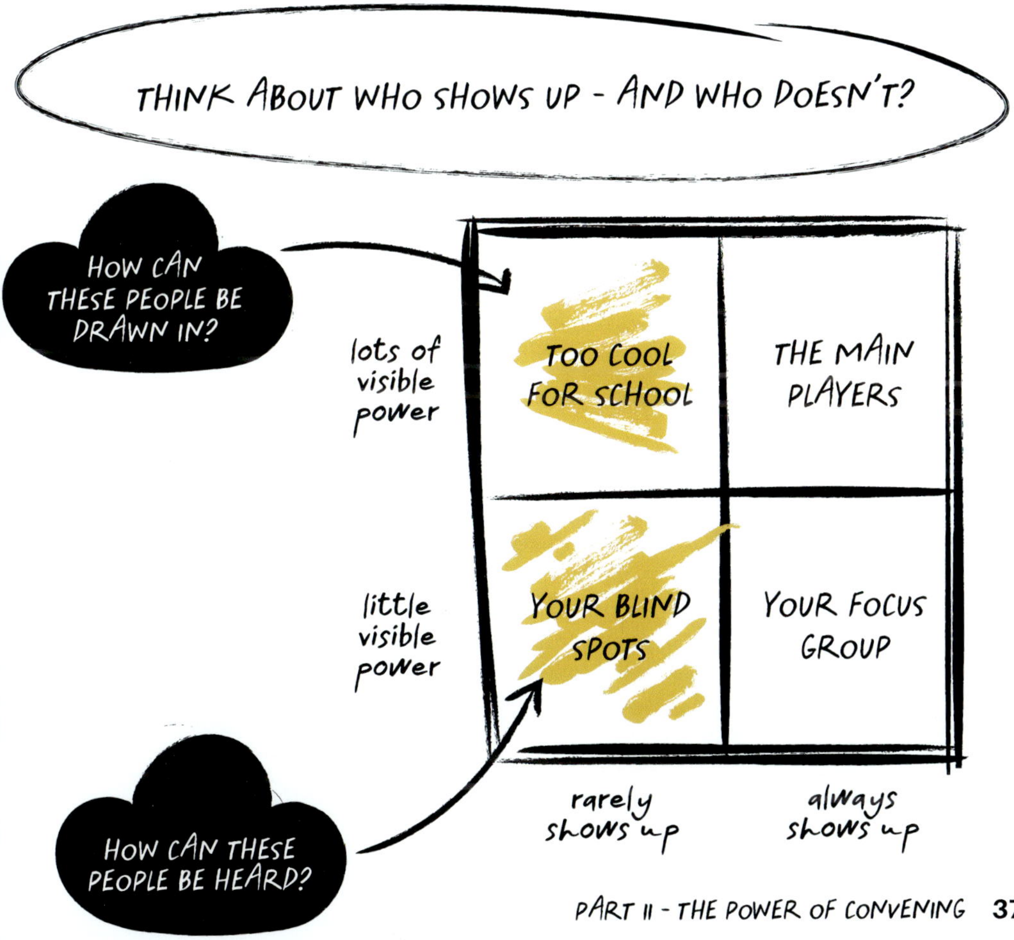

DON'T CONSULT. CONVENE

Another common model people reach for, consciously or unconsciously, when drawing up a list of invitees is the consultation model.

Use this picture to reflect a bit upon your own history of consulting with others.

- Who tends to be included in the decision-making around this topic?
- Who tends to be consulted (in other words, made to feel part of the decision)?
- Who tends to be excluded?

Put people or groups of people into those rings. Then **reverse the logics:**

THE PEOPLE WHO TEND TO BE INCLUDED?

Approach this circle **with caution**. It includes many of the usual suspects. They are already familiar with how you look at things, so the people in this circle may have less to offer you when it comes to helping you see the blind spots in the map you've drafted. When adding people to your list, the acid test for people from this circle is, *"Who here do I think is ready to brave a new way with me?"*

If people in this circle **do** pop out at you when you ask yourself this question, then you definitely do want to recruit them. If you do discover something new and important on this journey, they might become **allies** who help you show the rest of this circle the wisdom of what you have found together.

Don't go exploring alone. But don't go accompanied by so many allies that your own views become invulnerable.

THE PEOPLE WHO TEND TO BE CONSULTED?

Again, a good acid test for you to ask yourself is, *"Who is ready to try another way?"* With this group, that question means two things:

1. Who is ready to approach **this topic** in another way? And,
2. Who is ready to relate with **me** in another way?

The people in this group are used to being made to feel they've been consulted on a decision that other people have decided needs taking. Here, you are inviting them to join you at a much earlier (and more influential) stage, so that they can weigh on things like: *What decisions need to be made?* And even more fundamentally, *What questions do we need to be asking?*

THE PEOPLE WHO TEND TO BE EXCLUDED?

Here, the opportunity is to reevaluate who should and shouldn't be excluded.

The list of excluded people is boundless. You will probably exclude the vast majority of humanity from your invitation, and for good reason: they have **no genuine tension with your topic**.

Your goal is **not** to include everybody. In one special sense, you are convening an exclusive list of invitees. They are all people who are genuinely affected by this stuff you want to talk about. And when you say affected, you mean both:

1. Affected in the outward sense of "I am involved in this situation."
2. Affected in the inward sense of "I care about this situation."

A lot of people are affected in the outward way but not in the inward way. You can't know until you invite them. If they decline, that's fine. This is not a process to convince people that your topic is important to them. (But if it resonates, great.)

Nor is this a process for people who are affected in the inward sense but not the outward sense. There are a lot of "influencers" in the world today. Some of them take positions on topics with which they have no genuine relationship — just to grab attention. They're tourists to your topic. They have a "position on your issue" but not a "stake in your situation."

Do not invite topic tourists. They cannot help you explore a space they do not inhabit themselves.

DARE TO DEFINE DIVERSITY

When forming your list, at some point you'll probably start thinking about diversity.

Diversity is a big word. It's an emotionally and politically charged word. For your purposes, the key question to ask yourself is: ***Which* diversity is relevant to my topic?** Then be guided by your thoughts about that.

You can pack a room full of visibly diverse ages and races — who are all from privileged backgrounds. You can pack a room full of White people — ranging from the poorest of the poor to the richest of the rich. Which room is more diverse? Ask different people and you will get a different answer, depending on the lens they bring to such debates.

Which roomful of people can look at *your* map and better identify the terrain to be explored more? **That** is your lens. Which roomful of people can better enlarge everyone's view of the situation? That's the only diversity that concerns you here. As the genius of all this, dare to declare your own views regarding the **relevant** mix that is missing.

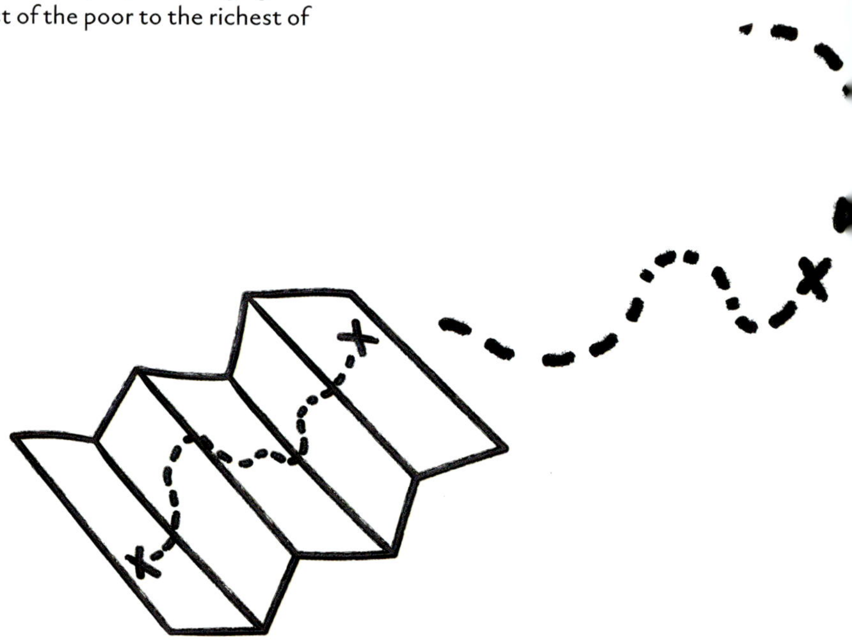

UNUSUAL SUSPECTS

If you've done some blunt stakeholder mapping and if you've critiqued your consultation habits and if you've dared to define diversity for yourself, you are already well on your way to convening a collection of perspectives that looks a lot less like the usual suspects and a lot more like the mix that is missing.

Your next step is to expand your list in exciting ways that will get everyone you invite (and you yourself) to immediately think, "I need to be part of THIS conversation."

A BIG QUESTION CANVAS

One lens on diversity that we have found to be really powerful in many cases is to think about the diversity of **questions** that you can convene.

Think of it this way. As a convenor, you make your impact by bringing different individuals into the here and now, together, to a single point of space-time.

So, one reliable way to make that single point a place for *expansive* conversation is to bring together people who **quest** in each of the four cardinal directions: in time, forward & backward; in space, outward & inward.

People on different quests tend to carry different questions into the here and now.

Time

People who have a strong forward orientation tend to contribute questions that offer a sense of direction.

People who put a lot of energy into exploring the past contribute questions that help you become conscious of wisdom, of ancestry, of your conversation's context, and of the origins of stories you are telling.

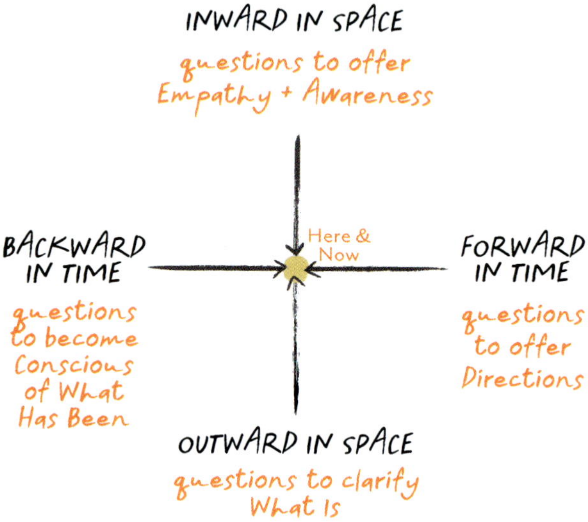

Space

People who orient outwards tend to bring questions that help clarify what *else* is *also* true, real, or happening.

And those who attune strongly to inner space bring questions to heighten empathy and awareness of our own relationships to the topic being talked about.

These four cardinal directions relate to four broad ARCHETYPES in society...

1. The LEADER or POLITICIAN explores the future.
2. The HISTORIAN or institutional administrator explores the past.
3. The SCIENTIST or PHILOSOPHER explores the outer world.
4. The ARTIST or POET explores the inner world.

Here's a simple table to help you think about WHO ELSE you might invite, to bring forth questions from each cardinal direction...

	INWARD	OUTWARD	BACKWARD	FORWARD
ARCHETYPES	artist, poet	scientist, philosopher	priest, historian, institution	leader, politician
DOMAINS	the arts	science	history	politics
SOURCE OF TRUTH	timeless, poetic beauty	rational judgement	wisdom	selection process
OFFERINGS TO THE HERE & NOW	empathy, awareness	clarity	consciousness	direction
BELIEFS	the inner is real	the outer is real	there's an origin	we have a destiny
WHAT'S REAL FOR THEM	emotions, metaphor	the senses, evidence	past experiences, memory	willpower, visions
WHAT'S VALID OR PERSUASIVE	feelings	reason, philosophy	ritual, ceremony	loyalty, achievement
WHAT'S AT STAKE HERE & NOW	our place in society	our place in the world	our place in history	our place in the future

The Big Question Canvas is one structured way you might think about diversity, not for diversity's sake, but for the sake of convening an unmissable conversation.

Right now, your draft may look to you like a flat sheet of paper. But bring together the right mix of people, and everyone will start to see its many layers more clearly and distinctly.

You want those **layers** to be revealed, because, let's face it: so many of the conflicts we are grappling with today are conflicts between these cardinal directions — conflicts between our inner selves and outer processes, conflicts between responsibility to the past and to the future.

You want to **make these tensions visible**, so that you can explore them. You don't want to bring together the skills and allies you'd need to take the actions you're ***already*** thinking of. You want to bring together the perspectives needed to discover actions you're not thinking of yet.

The best actions you could take are hiding between the layers.

HOW MANY PEOPLE SHOULD I INVITE?

How many people should you invite onto this journey with you?

The right answer is (inevitably!), **it depends**. Who all is affected by this? The members of your family? Your team? Your city or country or the world? The number of people you involve on this journey really does depend on the territory you want to explore.

Everything you are doing here is **scalable**. For our part, we've done this with small groups, with global corporations and at international music festivals. We don't think there really is any scale limit to these methods.

Your power to convene is limitless.

However large the total list of people you bring together, your gathering will include elements of whole-group interaction and small-group discussion. Bonfires and campfires.

However large your list, at some stage, small groups are going to get together because it is at that intimate level where people reveal the most and where revelations tend to happen.

Having said all that, consider the wisdom of **starting small**. If you are doing this for the first time, think more in terms of forming a scouting party than an expeditionary force.

Simplify the organisational burden of this (or ask the NewGeo community for help). Give yourself ample time and opportunity to experience the interpersonal dynamics of the campfire.

That way, when you do scale up to create the bonfire experience, you've already got personal familiarity with the intimate aspects of this journey.

Small is beautiful.

Small is necessary.

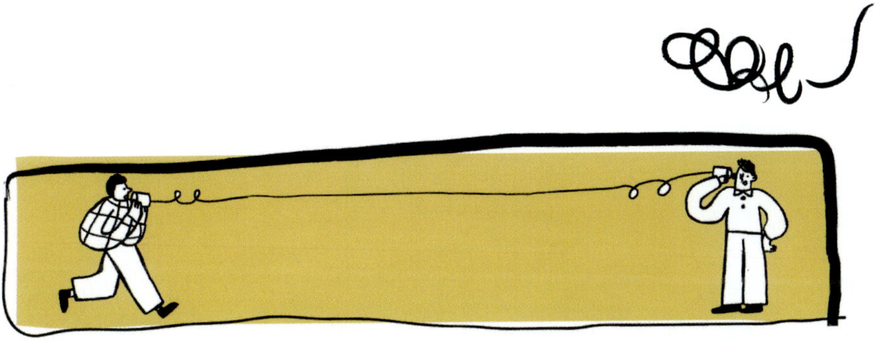

WHEN IS MY LIST DONE?

You'll know you are done compiling your list of invitees when you can look at it and honestly say three things:

1. This is **not** the usual suspects; this is a mix that's missing.
2. I **need** to be a part of this conversation.
3. I **want** to be a part of this conversation.

If these people come together around your topic, it's going to reveal things you can't see yourself. It's going to reveal uncharted territory that's worth exploring more. It's going to reveal new paths that are better than straight forward.

This would be a better beginning.

Do you believe that?

If yes, you're ready to keep going.

MAKING YOUR INVITATION

Now comes the part when you turn **me** into **we** — when you catch people in the midst of their busyness and invite them to pause and join you at a gathering place you've prepared for a conversation that might reveal new ways.

We've learned that a good invitation follows six principles...

SIX PRINCIPLES

1. *It's personalized.* Sending the same message to 15 recipients may save you time now, but it's less effective than sending that message to a single recipient, with a brief note that conveys: I've really thought about this and that's why I'm sending this to you.

2. *It's in your own voice.* On the pages 50–51, you can read an example of an invitation that I might write. You would write it differently. Maybe you'd break it into two or three messages. Do what's natural for you. It'll work out better.

3. *It's plain.* Use whatever medium feels right for you to make your invitation, but don't overproduce it. Plain text is better than a template. A conversation over coffee is better than a conversation in the boardroom. The stronger the formalities, the stronger the filter people apply to their own words and actions, and the less raw honesty we all bring to the conversation. So: signal your preference for informality in the form and language of your invitation.

4. *It's an invitation, not an obligation.* You only want people who are genuinely (i) affected, (ii) want to be part of this, and (iii) have the energy to join you on this journey. **Make it easy for the people you invite to say no.** Make it clear that they don't need to give you any particular reason for saying no. Maybe even offer them a formula for how to say no: "I'm sorry I can't take part, but I think it's fascinating and important what you're doing and I'd love to hear some outputs and insights once you've got them."

5. *Be conscious of your power.* Keeping a sense of obligation out of it can be hard to do when hierarchy is involved. It can be hard to say "No" to the boss. So if you're going to invite people below you in a formal hierarchy, the onus is on you to first check with yourself: Might I hold it against this person if they say "No" to my invitation? If so, don't invite them. If not, then do invite them, but take an extra moment to think about how to invite them in a way that tries to set aside your power differences.

6. *It's complete.* However you voice and format it, your invitation should answer these questions for your invitees:

- The situation or challenge: What is the situation that is prompting you to do this?
- The stakes: Why does it matter to you? Why might it matter to me?
- Your expectations, if I accept: What are you inviting me to do, exactly? If I say yes, what am I committing myself to do?
- The logistics: How would I do what I'd commit to doing? What's the process you have set up for me?
- The outcome: What's in it for me? What's in it for us?

HOW WILL YOU GATHER RESPONSES?

Decide how you'll gather responses.

"What did my draft evoke for you?" You'll want each person who accepted your invitation to answer this question. You want to capture their *individual* responses to your draft before their thinking can be influenced by seeing the reactions and responses that others have given you.

Consider composing a feedback form or a survey, which each participant can complete independently.

Your participants will appreciate a well-designed feedback form or survey that breaks their job of responding down into smaller parts. Bear in mind the practicalities of how they'll respond to your draft. With the best of intentions, they will probably block out one or two hours in their busy calendar. But when that moment comes, they will discover they don't have as much time available as they had hoped. They will pick up your draft with an urge to get it done, in between *finishing this thing* and, *oh yeah, that other thing that just came up...*

So make it easy for them to respond thoughtfully in the time that they have available. Offer some open-ended questions to help them bring their mind to the task quickly and to guide their attention in the different directions you think might be fruitful. Three good questions tend to be:

- What stands out for you?
- How is this similar to your own experiences? What's something you see differently?
- What's not clear?

Some people won't need your structure. They prefer their own and will ignore yours completely when offering their responses. That's great. Others will be grateful that you have taken the time to give them a good tool that helps them to get started and helps them to know when they're done.

*

A Note About Technologies

There are many technologies and tools you might offer to your participants to accomplish this phase of the journey. Email, Slack, Google Docs or maybe a virtual whiteboard.

The best tool is the one that works for everyone involved.

Beyond that one criterion, the success of this phase does not depend upon which technology you choose.

It depends mainly upon you being clear on

1. your role as curator, and
2. the signposts the curator needs to supply...

HERE'S A SAMPLE INVITATION

Hi Nancy,

I'm grappling with a big challenge that touches on a lot of things in our community, and I'm inviting a range of the people who may be affected by it to explore it more together and see where the journey takes us. I'd like to invite you to join this conversation.

Let me tell you a bit about what started this for me. In my role as community events manager for the library, I've got what feels to me like an unsolvable problem. As a library, two big values for us are intellectual freedom and inclusivity. But when it comes to holding public events and letting people in the community use the library to speak their own views, these two values are coming into conflict more and more often. For example: "Should we rent out our lecture theatre to a speaker who wants to promote anti-immigrant views?" There's no safe answer to questions like these, and it's constantly creating tensions for us and our readers. I'm starting to feel that it needs a much broader conversation than the one we've been having internally.

I feel strongly affected by this issue, in a number of ways. I'd like to invite other people who are affected by it, in different ways than me, into a process to talk about this stuff together. I think it touches on some big questions that can only be answered as a community, and I'd like us to make that happen.

I've taken some time put down on paper, in a structured way, how I'm looking at the situation today. I'm attaching that draft to share it with you. I'm also attaching a link to the guidebook I've decided to follow for this process. It's called HOW TO BASECAMP. It explains a lot more about what I'm trying to do, why it might lead to some fresh thinking and better alternatives, and how you can get the most out of the process.

I'm sending this invitation to about a dozen people. If you do feel affected by this, and if you have the energy for this, I'd love for you to be involved. Saying "yes" does come with a couple specific expectations, so please feel free to say no. No explanation needed. I'd be happy to share the outputs and insights, if you're interested.

My first expectation would be for you to react to my draft and help to improve it with how YOU see things. What do you agree and disagree with? What resonates and what doesn't? If you say "yes", my hope is that you will set aside at least one hour to read, reflect, and share with me your thoughts.

My second expectation would be for you to try your best to be available to meet up with me and everyone else who also says yes. I'll try to nail down a date and time that works for most people, but I'm aiming for the week of [DATE] and a full day of time together. At that "Basecamp", we will talk about this shared challenge in an informal, supportive atmosphere.

That's where my expectations end. After that, it's all hope! This guidebook I've been using, it talks a lot about this being a journey in three dimensions at once. And here I'm quoting the book:

"The first dimension is inward. It's about learning more about the assumptions that we are holding — of putting them out there, recognizing them objectively, and letting them just "be" without emotion tied to them. It's about discovering our own blind spots.

"The second dimension is outward. It's about learning more how other people see the world, and the experiences that have led them there. It's learning about their assumptions and how they hold them.

"The third dimension is toward each other. As each of us learns more about ourselves and new ways of viewing the world, a different, shared horizon can emerge — one that is greater than any of us could have imagined at the start."

I like that a lot. And I hope to explore all three dimensions with you. I want to discover some of my own blindspots so I can see the things that I'm not seeing right now. I hope to understand how you see things better, and I hope that you would also come out of this with some new ways to think about and impact some tough questions in our community. Finally, I'm hoping that one or more new groups might form up, as a result of our Basecamp, and decide to meet again and keep working on "shared horizons".

I'd like to figure out who will take part in this with me by [DATE]. For starters, could you please let me know your reactions to all this? I'm also happy to get on the phone and talk more about it.

Best,

Chris

Attachments:

MyDraftMap.doc

[HOW TO BASECAMP e-book link]

I'VE BEEN INVITED. NOW WHAT?

You've received a draft of somebody's map, and it came with this guide attached. Now what?

That's entirely up to you.

You might intuitively know what to do now. If so, follow that intuition. Or, you might want some more guidance on how you're expected to respond.

If it helps, think about your response as something that you craft on **three levels**:

Level 1 - Notice some things

Feelings: Just notice some of your initial feelings. Responses like: *Well, this was unexpected...* Maybe notice some curiosity: *Interesting... I wonder where this might go?* Or notice some doubt or skepticism: *Pfft. This won't go anywhere!*

Style: Notice the unusual style of leadership that is being attempted here: leadership by ***not knowing***. They are not saying with this, "Follow me!" They are not offering you a clear direction or an answer to a problem. Instead, they are saying, "There's something going on here that's bigger than I can see. Maybe we should get together around this?"

How does that style land with you?

Tone: Notice the tone of all of this. There's a lot of ***humility*** in their invitation. It's begun from a place of "There's a lot I don't know" and a belief that maybe not-knowing is the best starting point. There is an attitude of ***appreciation*** in their invitation. When part of the goal is to see one's own blind spots, it's impossible to know whom the key revelation will come from. Maybe it needs to come from you.

Generosity: Notice the generosity in their invitation. They have invited you because they need something: a better understanding, which you can help them achieve. Maybe you need that, too. Maybe what emerges from this will ultimately prove more useful to you than to them. And ***they are okay with that.***

Filters: Also, notice your filters. How you're receiving this invitation can't help but be influenced by how you see its sender. Does it come from someone lower in your hierarchy? Or higher? Does it come from someone with less power or influence or prestige? More? Does it come from someone you know well or someone you've never heard of? Notice the filters that have been activated in you by this invitation. Maybe now's a good time to filter differently. Or maybe not. ***Go with your gut.***

You are also now in a position to INFER two things about the person who sent you this invitation.

1. Clearly, this topic matters a lot to them. They have put some deliberate thought into this. (If you are curious to know just how much, feel free to skim the rest of this guide!)
2. Clearly, they think you might have something important to add. Their invitation to you was not idly sent. They think maybe you can see things that they can't, and they want your help to see those things.

Level 2 - Answer their invitation

At another level, you want to directly answer their invitation:

Do you want to be involved in this? Do you want to join this conversation?

The person who sent you this invitation had to make some assumptions about you. As part of your decision process, you want to check whether their assumptions are correct:

Are you affected by this? Their first assumption is that you, too, are affected by this topic: it has consequences for you, and you care about those consequences. Fundamental to this whole process is a shared sense of *in-it-ness*. This isn't a problem "out there" you can step back from and advise objectively; this is a *situation*, and (in different ways) you are all "in it".

You aren't being invited to help someone solve their problem. That's not what this is. You are being invited to help improve a situation that, in some way, you are in, too.

If you don't feel in some way: *Yeah, I relate to this situation* or *Yeah, this affects me as well*, then you should decline the invitation. You don't need to explain why.

It might be wise to decline *while opening a doorway*, so that if some really good stuff does come out of this, you can benefit and maybe contribute at a later date.

Do you have energy for this? Their second assumption is that you might have energy for this (which is different from having *time* for this). Does their invitation move you? Does the draft they've shared with you **unsettle** you, in a positive way? Do you want to explore what might emerge from this? If you feel entirely settled or feel no energy to go on this journey of discovery, then decline the invitation.

Trust your intuition. By this point, you should have a pretty strong feeling about whether you want to say yes or no to this. Go with that intuition. If it is to say "Yes", here are some thoughts about how to respond most helpfully to the draft map you've been given...

Level 3 - Improve their draft

If you're a "Yes", then you want to respond to their draft. They may have crafted specific questions that they have given you to think about, or you may decide to craft your own. One way you might think about how to respond to the draft you've been sent is to imagine that you and your inviter each stand in your own circle of vision, with some overlap between you, like this:

Their draft is their attempt to describe their circle. By sharing it with you, they've created three spaces for you to explore.

- **The overlap (resonance and conflict).** As you read their draft, ask yourself: What resonates with you? What strikes as strange or *That's just plain wrong* for you?
- **Your circle (what's clear to you).** What is missing from their map that you can see? What can you help to reveal for them?
- **Their circle (what's been missing for you).** Hopefully, the learning goes both ways. What has their map revealed to you? Is there something that they really pay attention to, that maybe you haven't looked at in the same way or to the same degree?

As you respond to their draft, you might want to run through these questions twice: once while wading into the details of what they've described, then again while stepping back and observing the whole landscape of what they've drawn and what they've not seen.

Choose the spirit of your response. Your response carries content. It will also carry attitude. It's helpful to take a moment and make a conscious choice about that, too.

It's going to be helpful if you approach this, not as giving feedback, but as **co-creation**. Someone had to start things off, but the end-goal is not to improve one person's private knowledge; it's to bring forth collective intelligence. You're not helping them to complete their picture; you're helping build a bigger picture *for both of you.*

You're helping to craft something that everyone who added to it can take something away from. The end-product may even prove to be more useful to you than to the instigator of this.

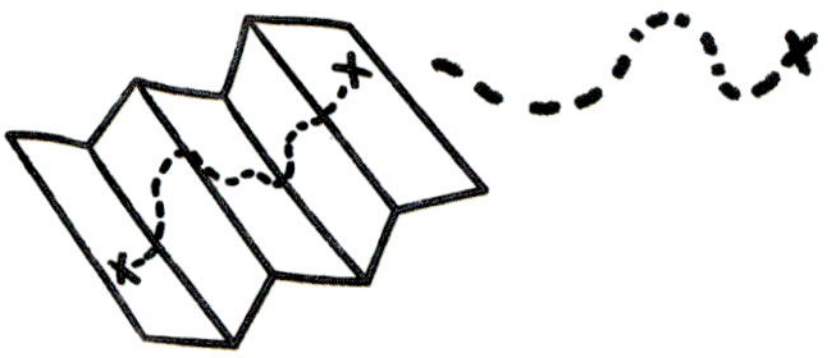

What if your two circles look to you like THIS?

Ask them - What were YOU thinking?

Ask the person who invited you to tell you more about their thinking. *I'm curious - Why did you invite* ***me****?* Do they see a relationship that maybe you don't?

Or what if your two circles look to you like THIS?

Again, ask them for more of their thinking. *What new perspective do you imagine I might be able to bring to this?*

HOW TO SURFACE TENSIONS

✳ In this phase, your role shifts from map-maker to conversation-curator.

Signpost conversations worth having

Wade into the rich mix of responses that your draft has evoked, and emerge from that mix with at least four **Signposts**, each one suggesting a different pathway to meaningful talk. These signposts will structure the conversation when you gather together at Basecamp.

For the moment, you want to look at everything you're getting back from your invitees and ask,

*Where do I see **tensions**?*

*Where do I see opportunities to **talk more**?*

Each Signpost is a conversation-starter. It comprises a **headline** that you'll craft, plus a **collection** of related statements that you'll curate (but won't edit, except for clarity).

Some of your headlines might be in the form of a question, since questions are natural conversation-starters. Or it might be that you cannot yet see The Question. In that case, your headline might simply name a topic.

The collection under each headline is a set of statements that you'll lift straight from people's responses *and from your original draft*. Each statement relates to the headline, but they don't all relate in the same way. Together each collection aims to make clear, **"I see a real conversation to be had among us here..."**

By placing your own words from your original draft alongside the responses of your invitees, you free the conversation from the constraints of your own frame. And you make it easier to explore dimensions that you couldn't have imagined when you began...

How You Arrive At Your Signposts Is Up To You. Here Is A 3-Step Process That Reliably Works For Others...

1. Look with a quantitative lens

Put together all the responses you've gathered. It's unlikely that every bullet point of your draft evoked equal interest from your invitees. So look for the patterns of hot and cold.

Heat: Where is there a lot of energy? Where are the hot-button parts of your draft that evoked a lot of reaction? Craft one or more conversation-starters to give that energy space to be explored more. What are we all reacting to? What are we all seeing? What are we all hearing? You'll probably find it easy to collect a variety of statements under that headline.

Cold: Now flip that lens. Where wasn't there any reaction? Where wasn't there energy *and you feel disappointed* by that? Are there some things you wrote that felt important or revelatory to you but didn't evoke any response from other people?

Dig there for another Signpost — this time, pointing at what we might be missing.

Why didn't anyone feel drawn to this? Is it because you all agree with me? Or is it so controversial that we can't begin to talk about it? What's going on here?

You might have a hard time finding supporting statements to put under this headline — and your headline can highlight that fact.

2. Look with a qualitative lens

The quantitative lens tends to reiterate the hot-button issues. We've been looking at things a certain way for so long, and those prevailing ways of looking at things are going to show up in the pattern of responses you get.

In your role as curator, you also want to bring a qualitative lens to the crafting of conversation-starters.

You want to do more than recreate the conversations people are already having.

So: What are the conversations we are **not having**? Forget patterns of hot and cold: Which responses **moved you** most? Which response did you see and instantly think to yourself, *I want to talk more about that!...?*

You sent your draft out into the world. What **unexpected** things came back at you? Which reaction hints at a totally new way or new frame? Which response unsettles you, because it suggests a whole other dimension to this topic you hadn't thought of?

What deserves more attention?

Signpost a conversation in THAT direction.

3. Look with an eye toward path-diversity

You might also find it useful to glance back at the Big Question Canvas (p.43). Most people tend to signpost conversations that aim mainly in the **outward** direction — exploring what is. Use this Canvas to diversify the paths that you and your invitees can travel together.

Remember: your draft is meant to start a multi-dimensional conversation. You've drafted a bit of your personal stake in this. You've drafted the background of where all this is coming from for you. You've drafted where all this might go. Curate your conversation-starters such that the people you've invited have the opportunity to explore more in each of these dimensions.

> Signpost a pathway that leads **inward:**
> What is our relationship to all this?
>
> Signpost one that looks **backward:**
> What have we done?
>
> Signpost a conversation that looks **forward:**
> What could we do?

Keep each of these paths open. It is too early to say where the biggest revelations will come from.

Optional options

Do you want to do a step 1.5?

You might choose to add an intermediate step, when you **reflect** everyone's individual responses **back** to everyone. You can then invite them to respond to the responses (which might make it easier for you to identify where the strongest tensions and energy lie). You might ask:

- What do they see emerging from across everyone's responses?
- What is interesting or surprising or disappointing to them?

Do you want co-curators?

Like your prior decisions of whom to invite, choosing a small number of conversation-starters is part of your genius. There is no right answer, so **let go** of the need to get your Signposts right. Only you can see the tensions and connections that you do.

You may want to invite one or more of your participants to join you in this task, to help you identify tensions and connections or simply to help you wade through the volume of responses. Do that if it feels right to you.

But don't be afraid to curate alone, either. This is not meant to be a democratic process. And your Signposts are conversation-starters, not -enders. You're crafting an agenda to get things started. Your invitees will have plenty more opportunity to steer things, too.

Do you want feedback on your signposts?

If it makes sense to you intuitively and logistically, you could share your Signposts with your group and check in with them: How good a job did I do of signposting conversations that you have energy for?

If no one has energy to go in a particular signposted direction, then you know this isn't the group to go that way. **Don't try to make them.** (Although you might take the time to share with them how you feel about that.)

And again, don't make this a quest for only the most popular topics of conversation. The smallest group, exploring in the loneliest direction, might bring back the most startling insights for everyone.

Part III, Where Brave New Ways Begin

"If we speak with each other as humans, we will figure it out. We can have [redacted] conversations and build societal structures that evolve beyond the limitations of the past."

WELCOME TO BASECAMP

It is important to **name** your act of convening. What you are hosting here is not a meeting; it's more like a gathering. It's not a discussion or debate; it's closer to a dialogue.

All these words get thrown about frequently.

To create a different space for people to arrive differently and engage differently, it helps to give **your** space a different name.

Yours is a gathering aimed at weaving collective understanding and bringing forth collective intelligence, to discover new ways that can only be found together.

You are going to attempt something that is not easy.

You're searching for something bigger than yourself. You're not here to "win", or even compete.

You need to work together as a team. You all bring different skills and knowledge, and you need to trust and rely on each other.

You will have a shared feeling of accomplishment if you succeed.

Our recommended name for this distinctive space is *Basecamp*.

The Meeting is the Midpoint

In today's world, much can be accomplished asynchronously. But you and your participants also need a dedicated time and space where you can come together, to be together and explore together in the here and now.

The meeting is the midpoint.

And it is central. It is where participants can fully embody their perspectives (of which the journey up to now has offered everyone only the barest of glimpses). It is where the mutual sharing of individual perspectives makes possible the discovery of shared purposes, questions, and tensions.

It is not a place to arrive at consensus or a joint communiqué. If the people who come together can accomplish that, they are the wrong people to come together for this.

It is where invitations to embark on new inquiries together are formed, made, and accepted — by some, but perhaps not by all.

HOLD SPACE LIGHTLY

You've invited people. They've accepted your invitation. You've signposted paths where there are tensions — energy! — to explore more. You've prepared a place to begin. Next, you need to design a process for arriving at a desirable outcome.

No, actually, you don't.

Not alone, anyway.

We have learned that groups should adopt the **minimum process needed**, and no more. A group of people who have never met, who come from different cultures or who speak different languages may need more structure (like an "ice breaker" segment or space for translators) than a group who have known each other for a long time. Basecamping with a group of 500 people is going to require more advance planning than basecamping with a group of 5.

Structure for conversations is a lot like a turtleneck. For some it provides great comfort; for others it feels (and looks) awkward.

So as part of your Basecamp preparation, you might invite participants to opt into a pre-arrival conversation to figure out what the structure will be.

Those who love structure will gladly show up and bring structure. Those who decline will bring a greater sense of flow to your Basecamp.

Wearing your convenor hat, you're happy to adopt any structure that:

1. Guides all participants through phases of Arriving, Exploring, Sharing, Inviting, and Closing,

and

2. Makes time for:

- Getting grounded and getting lost
- Being one large group and being many small groups
- Exploring form and content
- Going deep into the signposted directions and drawing connections between them
- Discovering new tensions that people have energy to talk and listen about
- Capturing and reflecting on brave new ways of thinking and acting
- Beginning well and ending well

✳ When you discover what works well in your context, remember to share that discovery with this wider community of inquiry.

The world needs your know-how.

WHERE IS BASECAMP?

We are all working hard on our own path, to summit the peak that we can see. Basecamp is where we come down off our individual mountains to **pool perspectives** and try to form a better map of the whole landscape.

You go to Basecamp with the intention to explore with others, not conquer. It is a space to disclose what you do know **and reveal what you don't**.

Basecamp implies a starting point — and you're hoping it will prove to be so, for three dimensions of travel:

- **Inward journey.** Learning more about the assumptions that you are holding: putting them out there, recognizing them, and letting them just "be" without emotion tied to them — so you can discover your own blind spots.
- **Outward journey.** Appreciating more how other people see the world and the experiences that have led them to that perspective. It's learning about their assumptions and how they hold them.
- **Collective journey.** As each of us learns more about ourselves and different ways of viewing the world, a different, shared horizon might emerge — one that is wider than any of us could have imagined when we started.

Basecamp isn't any one physical place. It is a space that you can summon for yourself wherever and whenever you sense the need to understand a "territory" collectively, to see it from diverse perspectives, or with diverse ways of seeing and knowing, so that new connections can form and different pathways emerge.

You can summon this space inside your organization, in your community, across your industry, and at every kind of gathering in the world.

"TO BASECAMP" IS ALSO A VERB

"You know what? We should basecamp this."

When you say that, you mean: Instead of attacking the route we already see or staying on this path we're already on, let's find a **better beginning**. Before we rush into repeating the past, let's bring forth collective intelligence and explore this territory better together, because I get the feeling that we're missing something big.

There's got to be a better way than the ways we're seeing right now.

CAMPFIRE CULTURE

The actual conversations at Basecamp happen around campfires. Again, "campfire" is a word to help everyone find a different mode of interacting with each other.

The symbolism of the campfire is ancient and universal. Many books and people and other resources can help you delve deeper into that rich symbolism.

Around a campfire, everyone should feel that:

- I am able to contribute
  (The conversation isn't "owned" by one or a few)
- I am heard
  (Everyone is actively listening)
- I am supported
  (I can be authentic, truthful, and vulnerable)

Over time, we have noticed and named a few distinctive qualities of a campfire. It helps to make these explicit for your participants. These qualities have proven helpful for us, across the hundreds of campfire conversations we have convened. (This list of qualities continues to grow.)

Drop your titles. Basecamp is a place to begin differently. "So, what do *you* do?" is how we often begin a conversation "out there", but it's a disappointing way to start a conversation around the campfire. Titles tend to reduce the possibilities for fresh conversation and trap us into established patterns of interaction. We tend to use information about people's titles to form quick judgments of them. So, a good way to stay open and stay curious about each other is to not know too much too quickly about what others do. By the time it comes out (and it will), it should add to the conversation, not reduce it.

Explore, don't conquer. In a campfire conversation, you stay out of problem-solving mode. The campfire is a time and space to explore — to learn more about the situation and our different relationships with it. Problem-solving comes later, after we've improved our understanding of what the real problem is.

Around the campfire is also a time for revealing honestly **how you see things**. (That's why the others are there, to hear your perspective.) But don't try to persuade people that your view is the right view or that your issues are the most important issues. It's not a conversation for winning converts, it's a conversation for gathering gems.

The person who best defends their own truth will leave empty-handed.

Reveal your feelings with your data. Around a campfire is a time for talking about feelings, not data. Data often informs people's feelings, but when you shift your focus to the feelings themselves, you will find more conversations worth having.

Instead of arguing the point, you can disclose why it matters to you. For example: "The data shows a rise in home break-ins." Annnnd...What does that mean for you? Does it mean...

- "More and more people in the community are losing their moral compass"?
- "People who are vulnerable are being targeted"?
- "A segment of the population is being neglected"?

The world's data is already in everyone's pockets. But I can only access your *feelings* if you reveal them.

Be brave. A campfire is a supportive space, but it's not entirely safe. We are out on the frontier, right now. To explore our differences we may need to venture into unfamiliar territory we don't know how to navigate. You're going to have to be brave.

We are different in a lot of ways. To have any conversation, we need to cross a minefield of potential misunderstandings. We can either tip-toe around all of them, or we can learn not to fear the mines. Uh-oh, I just stepped onto a landmine. Now what? Are you going to laugh at me? Are you going to judge me from your mountaintop?

Or can we talk about it?

Here is your chance to try the latter way. And it's okay to do it badly. Don't expect your words to mean the same thing to different individuals, unless you've first had a brave conversation with those same individuals to create shared meaning.

Be free. Every person is sovereign over their own time and attention. They should follow their energy. If you don't feel energy towards the topic or feel like this isn't where you need to be, get up and find the conversation you do need.

Revere silence. We are finding that there is a very strong relationship between the amount of silent time injected into a conversation and how impactful people say the conversation was for them.

That makes sense: you can only listen when you're silent.

TEND THE FIRE

Again, there are books full of specific tips for how to have deep conversation.

We've seen it work (and not work) when people decide to talk in a strict circle. Each person has a turn to speak; everyone has their turn to be heard without having to struggle to get a word in edgewise.

We've seen it work (and not work) when groups make a conscious habit of sitting in silence for a few breaths after each person finishes speaking.

Much better than imposing a particular set of behaviours upon your conversations, we find, is to set aside time to **talk explicitly about form**, instead of content. Make time upfront to talk together about what could make this conversation different from other conversations you've had. Look back at the description of campfire culture. Choose one quality to focus on. Decide together how you are going to express it through your behaviour.

More effective than struggling to keep in your head the best tactics and techniques is simply to notice that your conversation has those two dimensions: **form** and **content**.

A campfire isn't something you can "fire and forget"; it needs to be **tended**. We all bring our own meeting habits with us to Basecamp, and we won't simply flip into a new mode just because we talked about it once. We will forget where we are. We will slip back into more familiar modes of interaction.

It's like learning to meditate. When you notice your mind is wandering, that's okay. Recognize it, re-ground yourselves around the campfire, and continue.

As a group, take the time to tend your fire.

THE THREE RULES

Whenever we've met at Basecamp, we've only needed Three Rules:

1. Take Care of Yourself
2. Take Care of Each Other
3. Take Care of This Space

We recommend naming The Rules out loud at the beginning of the gathering.

Everyone has a responsibility to uphold all three, but we've never elaborated what they mean. Like the tools you use to give your conversation a "campfire" quality, the specific meaning of The Rules is determined by you, the participants. They are Your Rules, not Our Rules.

If in your dialogues you reach a moment when you feel, *Hey, we need to talk about what these rules really mean*, then you have a duty to say something like: "Can we take a moment away from our topic to 'tend the fire' for a bit?"

Saying this can be hard to do. The Rules are conversation-starters for the bravest of conversations.

GET GROUNDED

Before conversation begins, offer the group a gift -- a moment to pause together and shift focus to the here and now.

"Getting grounded" is a short-but-significant part of every Basecamp. It helps people enter into brave conversations with openness, expectation, and curiosity.

Here is one meditation that was developed by one veteran 'camper through dozens of campfires. It's not for everyone or every conversation, but it has proven very popular as one way for a new mix of people to **get grounded together**:

To start, take a moment to soften your gaze.

Close your eyes if that feels comfortable for you.

Now, take a deep breath...

Soften your shoulders...

Keep breathing deeply as we go on a journey of imagination.

To start, bring your focus to the center of your body.

Now imagine a softly glowing ball of light taking shape there, in the center of you. If you like, give this softly glowing ball of light a colour.

Feel how the light is warm and welcoming. It is new to you, yet somehow familiar.

Imagine this ball of light inside you growing until its soft glow surrounds your whole self.

Now you are walking among big trees. It is cool and dark except for the soft light that surrounds you.

And as you walk down a path that leads you deeper between the trees, you begin to see other points of light of different colours, different sizes, coming from other directions. All converging on a single flickering fire somewhere ahead of you.

Walking toward that fire you enter a clearing. You see it is a large campfire and notice the other points of light are all circling around it. They are all the people here with you at Basecamp.

As we all draw around this campfire, our lights mingle until, together, we become one multi-colored circle around the fire.

You remain you, and at the same time you discover that you can expand your awareness to the whole circle. And although you only walked one path to get here, somehow you can now feel every path into this clearing. You can feel the whole forest, through the power of previously unknown connections.

Take another deep breath and - when you're ready - open your eyes and ears.

Welcome to our conversation.

Welcome to Basecamp.

TELL STORIES

After a period of exploration, the time will feel right to progress to a period of **consolidation**.

In the consolidation phase, small campfires (if there are any) rejoin the big campfire. The conversation shifts from exploring many pathways to coming together to tell stories of new discoveries and shared understandings.

The convenor's original draft map had 5 sections, and in this phase of your Basecamp, you want to invite revelations about them all. Recall the five sections:

1. **Context:** How did we get here?
2. **Challenges:** What do you see as the biggest challenge that we face right now?
3. **Pathways:** What are possible ways forward?
4. **Beliefs:** What beliefs shape how you understand the situation?
5. **Personal Intentions:** Why are you here? Why is this topic important to you?

But now the task is no longer for each participant to respond to your draft. It's for each participant to notice any changes in how they themselves see things, and to tell stories about their insights. Their discoveries.

- What has changed about your understanding?
- What did you realise in yourself?
- What did you realise from others?

It's also time to add three new sections to the map, and tell new, shared stories around those. These shared stories can only be drafted collaboratively:

- **Shared Purpose:** What themes keep coming up that we should capture and explore? Who feels a sense of purpose emerging from these conversations?
- **Shared Horizon:** What are some common futures that we (or some of us) feel pulled toward, even though our paths for getting there and specific visions may differ?
- **Shared Tensions:** What question are we not (done) asking, that we (or some of us) still want to explore? What tensions have we uncovered that are important to us?

This last one is crucial. **Do not push for an artificial consensus.** Don't suffocate dissonance. Give it space and value it. Gather the tensions. Those tensions can be a font of energy for further conversation, exploration, and discovery.

People who are in perfect alignment have nothing left to talk about.

NOTICE AND NAME WHAT'S EMERGING

By now, some things may be clearly emerging. Basecamping your challenge or situation often results in:

- Greater self-awareness
- A greater sense of empathy and compassion
- New and deeper relationships between people
- New and deeper relationships with a situation
- New realizations and understandings
- A deeper appreciation of a topic
- Unexpected energy towards a topic or direction

You may arrive at a richer, deeper, expanded understanding of your own situation, which helps you see paths you had never before considered.

You may spark a unity of purpose among other people, which you don't personally feel energized to take part in. Or you may feel part of it. You may feel energized to talk more about the unresolved tensions you feel amongst yourselves.

Name these things.

Any and all of them are a **better starting point** for whatever you decide to do next.

And remember, the best outcomes are UNEXPECTED.

DEBRIEF

While you're all still together and the experience is fresh, don't miss the **learning opportunity** of a Debrief. Your Basecamp comprised two levels of conversation: form and content. You've drawn implications from the content. Now take some time to draw lessons from the form.

- What worked for people? What didn't?
- In what ways did we manage to create the qualities of a campfire?
- When did it feel like the conversation turned into something else?
- How might we do things differently next time?

Log these learnings. Basecamping is hard. (That's why it's worth doing, even badly.) We're trying to interact in a different way with different people. And none of us is an expert at that. So add what you've learned from your attempts to the knowledge pool of the global community of inquiry that works with this guide.

Debriefing also opens an additional dimension of skill development for all participants. Through this process, you all practice skills that are crucial to navigate the new world well: reframing how we see things, understanding different perspectives, and being able to work with them. So take the time to consolidate those learnings.

DECAMP WELL

As a society, we are strongly conditioned to **prize action** and **devalue talk**.

Part of the broader change you are working in the world by convening Basecamp is to rebalance those biases. We should notice where more talk really is needed and **create space** for that. That's more impactful than busyness masquerading as action — i.e., doing more and more of the same sorts of things that have produced the situations that frustrate us.

But you can't prevent a strong "Less talk, more action!" bias from being present at Basecamp. It'll be there.

Acknowledge it and work with it.

People who are strongly action-oriented need to know that all this talk is building toward a phase of Decamping, when new expeditions might form up.

Make invitations

In this phase, participants shift from telling their stories to making invitations around the stories that have emerged: shared purpose, shared horizon, or shared tensions.

Ideally, the first invitation will come from you, the instigator. We've learned that this works well. It gives everyone else a very clear template for how to turn the conversation that you've been having into new invitations...

For example, I, having convened people at Basecamp to talk about the rising tensions between freedom and inclusivity at my library, might make an invitation this way:

"Do you know, when I did my original draft for this Basecamp, I was thinking mainly about how the library is struggling with the politicisation of its own space. But now it's clear to me that this is a much wider thing.

We are all struggling with how identity politics is politicizing our workplaces and how to respond to that. And I know there are some strong tensions about that here, some strong disagreements about what the problem is, or even how to name it and talk about it. It's clear to me that we've got some different visions about the end-state solution, too.

But I'm also hearing that there's a shared horizon that we'd all like to move towards, which is to have a healthier way of processing our identity politics. So I'd like to explore that more, and I get the sense that some of you might have energy for that, too. Would any of you like to go deeper into that question with me?"

Different people will feel differently towards each particular invitation. Some people may feel very deeply about its purpose. Others may agree that it is compelling but don't have the same passion for it. And that's okay. It should be made clear to everyone that saying "Yes" to these invitations is purely optional, and the #1 criterion should be inward: **Am I authentically energised by it?**

What other invitations are emerging?

Maybe Luna follows my example with this:

"You know, I came to this conversation thinking along those same lines, Chris — that we've just got to get a better handle on how to navigate identity politics, now that every space is a political space.

And I do still think that and I'm really interested to know what comes out of that group, so please do keep me in the loop.

But what this Basecamp has really opened up for me is a whole other dimension to this that I hadn't seen at all before. It's not the tension between politics and the workplace. It's more like the tension between the secular and the sacred. And I've just been exposed to this so I'm not even quite sure what I mean by that. But I really feel there's something big there and I want to explore that: How do we help the secular and the sacred to coexist better? If anyone else would like to explore that more with me, I'd welcome it."

And I might think to myself, *That sounds interesting, but personally I'm not really interested.*

And that's okay, too.

The invitations that emerge from your Basecamp might exclude you. In that case, you've done something good for the world. This began with you hitting a dead-end. Now it's become a wellspring of new beginnings for other people.

Who knows what all you've put into motion?

LOG THE JOURNEY

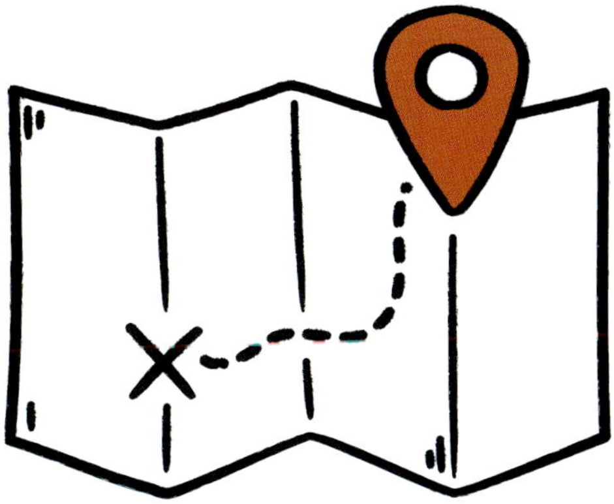

There is one formal output of Basecamp for which the instigator is responsible: a **logbook** of the journey up to now. In the days or weeks afterwards, it should be distributed to all participants.

It should have five components:

1. Your revision of your draft "map", improved and expanded by the discussions it sparked. (But remember, it's still only a draft, so it's ok if it's a bit messy. Life's like that.) If you haven't already, now is a good time to find an online collaboration tool to host your map, so that the other participants can add their experiences and insights to whatever you have captured.
2. The new sections of shared story that came out of the consolidation phase: Shared Purposes, Shared Horizons, Shared Tensions & Questions.
3. The learnings identified during the Debrief.
4. A log of any invitations made to each other before you Decamped and the groups that have formed around them.
5. A note of gratitude to all involved.

If you decamped with a group around you who've accepted your invitation to explore more together, then this logbook will be an essential shared starting point for that onward journey.

But if you yourself do not proceed beyond this point with this group of 'campers, it's still important to cause your logbook to be produced and distributed.

It's a product of collective intelligence, and the world needs more of it.

Conclusion - The World Needs Guides.

Now, You Are One

Leaders **are** lost. Navigating out of one crisis seems to land us into the next one. Trust in public institutions is at an all-time low. Too many people feel disempowered, disengaged, and unheard.

Awareness, education, entrepreneurship, and leadership alone are not going to get us where we need to go. We don't need more of what worked in the past; we need a fundamental rethink of how we move forward.

There have got to be **better ways**. But:

- It requires bravery to choose a different, untrodden path.
- It requires bravery to get to the heart of issues — and each other.
- It requires bravery to follow, to support, to go together.

In short, the world needs **guides**.

And now you are one.

By practicing *How To Basecamp*, you have demonstrated and you can help others understand that:

- **We need to reframe.** We need to stop trying to defeat our problems and learn to leverage them to reimagine our world.
- **We need to begin better.** We can expand our horizon beyond our current limitations, fears, and entrenched beliefs.
- **We need to gather differently.** Some things, we can only see together. We must meet a complex world with collective intelligence. And we can bring it forth, **if** we create a supportive space to probe, sense, reflect, and create together.
- **We need to brave new ways.**

By practicing How To Basecamp, you have discovered and demonstrated a brave new way to learn from one another and move together.

LET NEW JOURNEYS BEGIN

If you haven't already, share your story with NewGeo and with our global community of inquiry. *How To Basecamp* is a collective gift to the world, and you are now in a position to make it better.

Please do so.

Drop a note to **stories@newgeo.org** and tells us your story of what happened.

You came here looking
for a better way.

You leave as someone
who can help others
find it.

About the Author

Dr. Chris Kutarna is the founder of NewGeo. His passion is to explore the many possible futures of politics, business, society, and life, together with you.

Chris' first book, *Age of Discovery*, was an international bestseller, acclaimed for its startling foresight into the upheavals of the 21st century.

In *How to Basecamp*, Chris distills a decade of practice into a practical guide for leading transformational conversations—inside teams, companies, communities, and beyond.

He lives in London, but his real address is: around the campfire.